IT'S RAINING CLIENTS
FIND THE RAINMAKER INSIDE YOU

*A Lawyer's Guide to Originating Clients
with Ease and Grace*

HOWARD WOLKOWITZ

IT'S RAINING CLIENTS
FIND THE RAINMAKER INSIDE YOU

*A Lawyer's Guide to Originating Clients
with Ease and Grace*

Cover and book design by David Bricker.

ISBN: 978-0-9971042-0-2

"A wise man knows *everything*,
a shrewd one, *everybody.*"
—Chinese proverb

INTRODUCTION

No matter how great your command of the language is, how great your skills are, how great your knowledge of the law is, and how great your attitude is, it won't make a difference if you have no one to tell your story to.

This book will teach and inspire you to:

1) Identify the distinctions between working *in* your practice and *on* your practice.

2) Develop business through market segments.

3) Understand the importance of a marketing plan.

4) Create your brand.

5) Understand the difference between marketing and originations.

6) Understand the difference between a practice and a business.

7) Realize returns on business development investments.

IT'S RAINING CLIENTS
FIND THE RAINMAKER INSIDE YOU

Whether you are just beginning your practice or have been practicing for a while, creating your own clients can be fun and it can be scary. Reaching outside your comfort zone can create anxiety.

This lawyers' guide is about confronting what's scary. The moment you sign your first client, the results and fun of rainmaking begin.

A rainmaker is:

- A person who makes things happen.
- A person who brings in business.
- A person who develops relationships.
- A person who has established a reputation for honestly and integrity.

This book assists lawyers with staying ahead of the business development curve. Progressive law firms recognize that the need for continued growth mandates that their lawyers become more than technicians; the pursuit of continuous revenue streams is critical. In a world of commoditization, personal relationship development and building networks is essential to creating and maintaining clients and business.

As with many businesses, the roles of lawyers have evolved over time. With the advent of technologies such as Google and LegalZoom®, competitive pressures on service models and fees have grown.

The importance of business development originators in law firms has never been greater. Lawyers have long recognized that although they may be astute at law, they may not be as adept at cultivating business. Yet, when asked which attorneys make more money, have more control of their business, have more job security, and command the respect of colleagues in the firm, the answer is always the same: "The relationship masters."

In the world of business, originators are entrusted with a firm's most important asset: clients. Originators are the face of the firm. They are the ones who manage the branding process.

Client development is a career asset management strategy. Your career is an asset. A managing partner of a law firm summed it up: "There are two types of lawyers: lawyers who work for other lawyers, and lawyers who work for clients." One creates income; the other *wealth*.

In the legal industry, business development has grown into a job classification. Networking is one of the best tools for business development. It develops relationships that lead to strategic alliances that create referral business. Many attorneys think they want to have their own clients, but never take the associated actions.

Not all attorneys are comfortable networking or asking for business. The reasons vary:

> *"It looks like I am begging for work."*

> *"They know what I do. If they need me, they know where to find me."*

> *"It will look like I need the business."*

> And the all-time winner: *"I didn't go to law school to be a salesperson."*

Though business development can be profitable, not everyone is interested in being a business owner and/or business generator. It takes a lot of time, energy, and a commitment to develop business and that means time away from family attending events, conferences, dinners, etc.

When attorneys say they are not salespeople, what are they actually saying? Are they saying they do not want their own clients or are they saying they are not willing to invest the time, energy, and expense to develop business? Many lawyers are content to work with clients from other lawyers and understand the tradeoff between money and quality of life.

These "client service technicians" are critical to the practice of law. They support business originators in living the firm's brand commitment and delivering quality legal services. For attorneys interested in pursuing clients, the professional technology of creating business is both an art and a science.

MEASURE EFFECTIVENESS

Effectiveness is a result of a combination of intentional, actionable and coordinated activities performed consistently over time. It's easy to spend money developing business; the key is to have a high level of results without a corresponding high level of expense.

(ROI) RETURN ON INVESTMENT

ROI represents results versus investment. ROI can mean spending $5000 to sponsor an event or function where you obtain a new client who you bill $20,000. ROI can also mean spending $500 to join an organization where over the next year, you create new clients and bill them $20,000. ROI is a direct cost-benefit relationship.

(ROT) RETURN ON TIME

ROT is a vertical model. Vertical networking is narrow and deep. Vertical networking is about getting deeply involved in only one or two organizations. You become personally involved and more intimate with members. You develop more meaningful conversations and hopefully more trusting relationships. Vertical networking usually pays higher returns on time invested.

Horizontal networking is wide and shallow. When your model is a horizontal networking model you are involved in several organizations as an attendee only. Horizontal networking is usually superficial, not focused and intentional, and not as effective.

(ROR) RETURN ON RELATIONSHIPS

When someone who knows, likes, and trusts you

says, "I didn't know you did that," your ROR on that relationship is zero. You friends and family may know you are a lawyer, but this will not help your career if they have a problem, and you are not associated with the solution. Make sure people in your circle know what you offer.

(ROL) RETURN ON LEVERAGE

Leverage is about positioning yourself as a resource and a solution provider. Once you are known as a resource, people will reach out to you for direction and advice. Your return on being a resource will be more referrals and introductions because people feel safe and confident asking you to help them. Return on leverage can also occur when attorneys create referrals to other lawyers in the firm.

(DOA) DEAD ON ARRIVAL

Many attorneys attend events and spend their time hanging out with their buddies. They play it safe, don't extend themselves, and may even leave pretending like they accomplished something. Some are terrified at being in a room of strangers and are happy when the event is over so they can leave. As far as being effective marketers, these attorneys are dead on arrival.

MOMENT OF IMPACT

Events happen in life that require an immediate call to action. Often, when a person suddenly needs an attorney, even though they know several attorneys, they will ask others for referrals. At that moment of impact when a person needed a lawyer, why do they ask for referrals? The reason is because they lack the confidence in the people they know.

When this happens, consider it a breakdown in your communication and brand management.

SOURCE AND CREATE YOUR OWN CLIENTS

- Do what it takes to develop your own clients.
- Develop an ideal client profile.
- Identify organizations that have your ideal clients as members.
- Create an action plan to create meaningful relationships with ideal clients.

MAKE CLIENT CREATION A PRIORITY

- See yourself as a business originator.
- Become comfortable meeting and greeting new people.
- Learn to ask others for business or referrals.

DO WHAT IT TAKES

- Commit to spending smart time away from your family to prospect.
- Develop a process to source and create new business.
- Constantly ask for business.

DEVELOP AN IDEAL CLIENT PROFILE

- Know your core expertise and the profile of your ideal client.
- Learn the best places to meet your ideal clients.
- Be able to quickly explain the value you bring to your ideal clients.

IDENTIFY IDEAL NETWORKING ORGANIZATIONS

- Be clear about your unique value proposition. "I am an attorney," or "I am an estate planning attorney," doesn't say enough about your uniqueness and value.
- Be sure the organizations you affiliate with include people you really want to meet. Do your research before you commit to joining an organization.
- Regularly attend ideal events and *participate*. Business development is a contact sport. Participation is critical to obtaining results.

BUILD YOUR OWN ADVISORY GROUP

Find like-minded energetic leaders and networkers. Do fun things together, share contacts, discuss opportunities and be there for each other. Great teammates watch each other's backs.

Create your own business networking group and choose your teammates. Create an agenda of what you are up to and whom you want to meet—a specific person or type of professional, or someone from a particular company.

Create a memorable value proposition that will be remembered by advisors and customers.

Leaders know that customers don't buy legal services; they buy solutions to legal problems.

Create a simple Vision Statement for yourself:

My expertise is in ___and my ability to ____ is very valuable to my clients.

Creat a Mission Statement for yourself:
I will have one lunch per week with prospective centers of influence.
I will attend at least one target event per month.

LISTEN FOR OPPORTUNITIES

While most lawyers are astute *technical* listeners, many are not trained to listen for business opportunities. Some people call this social listening. Many focus only on the specific tasks at hand without developing the rapport with a client that enables them to provide a true value-added service.

Attorneys must be more to their clients, prospects, and friends than legal service providers.

A successful attorney-client relationship is built on clients thinking of their attorney not only when they need legal services, but also when they have other needs. Attorneys must learn to think of their clients not only with regard to providing legal services.

Attorney's help solve non-legal problems and open doors to new opportunities. By becoming "trusted advisors," they create or refer legal and other consulting services.

Part and parcel of listening for opportunities is recognizing the resources your firm makes available through its staff, clients, and the relationships it maintains in the community. The firm's attorneys must be aware of all the lawyers within it, regardless of which offices they are situated in and which areas of practice the firm's major clients are associated with.

Educating the lawyers within a firm about resources beyond themselves and the people with whom they regularly interact is critical to success at growing a business. Lawyers should be able to distinguish their firm's abilities or unique value proposition in a brief conversation.

CENTERS OF INFLUENCE

Centers of influence are professionals who establish "know you, like you, and trust you" relationships with others. They can be attorneys, bankers, brokers, advisors, CPAs, and business consultants. The art of business networking is about becoming a center of influence by learning to recognize and engage new distribution outlets.

- Determine who your best referral sources are.
- Meet with each of them to determine what you can do for them.
- Explore what clients you may have or want to pursue jointly.
- Find out how you can be a resource for them and their clients.
- Send them articles of interest.

BE KNOWN IN YOUR COMMUNITY

When your name is mentioned in a room, make sure at least one person in that room knows you. Start to build a presence as a community participant, community leader, and most importantly as a community giver. Give time, money, energy, services and leads to others. If you are going to be known, be known as a community giver, not as a community taker.

Your ideal clients are always nesting in plain sight.

ETHICS, ORIGINATIONS, AND MARKETING

Ethics, originations, and marketing can co-exist for lawyers.

Outside of law, people think of ethics as fair, equitable, and just dealing. People who are considered ethical by others conform to a self-imposed higher standard. No one needs to tell them to or how to be ethical.

As a member of the legal profession and as a representative of clients, you provide advisor, advocate, negotiation, and evaluation services. Originations and marketing can happen in an ethical way by understanding what your unique value proposition is and by sharing that unique value.

Ethical Marketing is a philosophy, not a strategy or a tactic. Successful marketing is about eye-to-eye relationship development. It's about being open, honest, and providing truthful, non-manipulative information. Ethical attorneys market *relationships,* not products and services. People don't care how much you know; they want to know how much you *care*.

ETHICS

A lawyer is a member of the legal profession, a representative of clients, an officer of the legal system, and a public citizen having special responsibility for the quality of justice. As a representative of clients, a lawyer performs various functions:

As an advisor, a lawyer provides the client with an informed understanding of his legal right and obligations, and explains their practical implications.

As an advocate, a lawyer zealously asserts the client's position under the rules of the adversary system.

As a negotiator, a lawyer seeks a result advantageous to the client but consistent with the requirements of honest dealing with others.

As an evaluator, a lawyer acts by examining a client's legal affairs and reporting about them to the client or appropriate others.

Whatever types of legal services you provide, remember that ethical business development revolves around the commitment you made to your client when you originated the relationship. Build your practice on a foundation of ethics and integrity to attract clients who expect professionalism and are willing to pay for it. When clients hire you, they are also hiring your brand promise.

ORIGINATIONS

An origination is a transaction between two parties where the client receives legal services in exchange for money. Originations are the process of converting a *potential* client into an *actual* client. Outside of law, people think of originations as selling.

MARKETING

Marketing is the activities associated with selling a service. Marketing cultivates awareness and draws potential clients toward you. Marketing is everything done to acquire clients and maintain relationships with them.

We may think we are marketing when we tell people who we are and what we do. Marketing is more than telling; it is a message to the marketplace that *positions* your practice. Marketing can appeal to a broad or narrow niche. Marketing positions you as the "go-to" expert on a particular practice area.

LIFESTYLE MARKETING

Develop business as a *lifestyle!* Brand yourself as the *"go-to source"* for providing legal solutions inside your field of expertise. Relationship building takes time; make it fun.

- Merge your passions with your business. Promote yourself within your ideal market.
- Get involved in causes and organizations you love.
- Build marketing outreach around your family's events, organizations, and associations dear to your heart and interests.
- Build marketing around your community leadership role, perhaps by being a board member.
- Prospect with a purpose. Before you attend functions, research the specific people who will be there. Determine who and how many people you want to meet. Do you want to meet CPAs, insurance agents, stockbrokers, or business owners?

YOUR MARKETING PLAN

Your marketing plan is critical to determining and delivering your message through every aspect of your communication with both clients and prospects. Your marketing plan is also critical to the cost effectiveness of your marketing efforts. Without a plan, how will you be able to determine if your strategies, messages, and actions are properly aligned?

Steps to creating your marketing plan:
- Identify your niche
- Position your practice
- Develop your marketing plan and budget
- Track your results and make adjustments

Your marketing plan should tell your community who you are and *why* you do what you do. They don't care *what* you do because endless lawyers do what you do. Explain your qualifications along with your offerings:

> *"I am a special needs parent who focuses on special needs planning."*

> *"I am an adopted child who specializes in adopting children."*

> *"I am a parent who experienced infertility who represents parents interested in infertility and estate planning."*

A tagline can be:
- Estate Planner: *"See Me Before You Go."*
- Criminal Lawyer: *"See Me Now or in 20 years."*
- Personal Injury Lawyer: *"Let's Not Meet by Accident."*

- Labor and Employment Lawyer: *"We Practice Safe Employment."*

Your marketing plan should include a calendar and a budget. It can be as simple as having a dedicated lunch each week with potential clients, or joining, attending, and taking on a leadership/sponsorship role in an organization.

Develop your marketing plan to address market segments. Are your customers:

- Individuals?
- Small, medium, or large businesses?
- Private or public companies?
- Not-for-profit or for-profit companies?
- Litigation or transaction clients?
- One-time clients or ongoing clients?
- Other professionals?
- Other attorneys?

Your marketing activities will vary depending on your answers. If you are interviewing for a job or presently hold a job, the following questions will be helpful in determining the support you will receive from your employer:

- What community organizations are the firm presently involved with and why?
- What relationships and opportunities have already come from these organizations?
- Is there a marketing budget for engaging with these organizations and others?
- Is there a formal associate development program that trains, coaches, or offers internal business development support?

Branding and marketing is *not* originating.

Branding and marketing is *passive;* originating is *active.*

Marketing is what you do *before* you meet someone.

Originations are what you do *when* you meet someone.

Marketing professionals design strategies by focusing on analysis and process.

Marketing involves branding, and originations involve living the brand.

Origination professionals focus on cultivating relationships and clients.

It's all about helping others; succeed by helping others succeed.

PROFESSIONAL BRANDING

Brand image is how the market thinks of you. For you to create a personal brand, the marketplace must see you as a solution for specific problems. Brand identity is how you *want* the market to think of you. When creating a brand identity, it is important to brand yourself as experienced and versed in a particular area. When a need for that specific area of expertise, service, or solution arises, you become the "go-to" person.

State your uniqueness in 25 words or less.

"I am unique because ... "

BUSINESS ORIGINATING IS A CONTACT SPORT

People play professional sports to win, not for the exercise. There is only one winner in professional sports and in business: the person or team who wins or the person or firm who gets hired. Business and sports are competitive, relentless, and unforgiving. In business you either get hired or someone else gets hired. If your career was a sporting event, the following might underscore your marketing strategies:

- The game I am playing is _____.
- I have the home court advantage because_____.
- I know the rules of the game I am playing.

- I have a plan to win this game.
- I put resources where results need to be generated.
- I am passionate about my plan.
- If an opportunity opens up, I will go for it even if it is not in my plan.
- If my initial plan doesn't work, I will quickly revise it.
- I know they keep score. I will focus on results and not on my intentions.
- I know my competitor wants to win, also.
- I take full responsibility for my plan and the results it produces.

BRANDS CREATE COMFORT

Before you create your brand, you must create your own uniqueness. A uniqueness is a way of defining how you appear to a client or prospect and what you are committed to. The way people see you and treat you is a function of the perceptions they have of you. Perceptions tell us where we can and cannot count on you.

YOU AS A BRAND

Thought leaders and rainmakers understand the value of personal and professional branding. You have a *personal* brand and your firm has a *professional* brand. Your brand defines who *you* are, what *you* want to be, and ultimately how you want people to perceive *you*. Your brand is what you communicate verbally and in media.

Building your personal brand is also about connecting to people and the community as a person. The more you give to your community, the more it gives back to you. Community involvement introduces you to like-minded people who open up opportunities for socializing and provides venues to get to know each other without the pressures of work.

- A *personal* brand is your reputation in the community and marketplace.
- A *professional* brand is your firm's reputation, an extension of your personal brand.
- Brands have key messages, slogans, phrases, taglines, images, and looks. A brand has a voice. Your brand could be "big firm muscle," "boutique concierge service," or "the expert's expert on ____."
- You can also brand higher fees/ higher quality or lower fees/higher value (but not both).

A brand represents a company's culture and your personality, beliefs, and actions. Brands are promises. A brand promise establishes what your client can expect from you and your firm.

Is your firm or are you considered an expert in a particular area(s)?

What differentiates you as an attorney? Why should I hire you?

BRAND BEING A THOUGHT LEADER

A thought leader is usually a person whose views and opinions are accepted as authoritative and influential. Thought leaders are recognized and respected in the crowded field of law. Thought leaders are seen as "go-to" sources in their areas of expertise. Their visibility is increased. They are usually accepted as both knowledgeable and influential. They move and inspire people with innovative, creative, and disruptive ideas. When the media wants an opinion on a controversial issue, they reach out to thought leaders. Being quoted assists in building a brand.

ACTION STEPS TO BEING A THOUGHT LEADER ORIGINATOR

- Arrange introductions, referrals, and recommendations for *others*.
- Get involved with organizations at the *leadership* level.
- *Join* strategic networking groups, trade organizations, and referral alliances.

- *Create* intimate client events, lunches, dinners, and social events.
- *Track* and celebrate your successes.

Originations and business development have several components. If you bypass any of the steps, you run the risk of not achieving your intended outcome, which is having more clients. Business comes from people knowing, liking, and trusting you. The steps are:

- **Getting to know you:** Engage in social conversations that allow you to relate to others on a personal basis.
- **Getting to like you:** Be yourself. Find areas of common interest and passions in conversations. Do not present yourself as a lawyer yet, but as a member of the community with a family, hobbies, and interests.
- **Getting to trust you:** Consider the criteria others use to decide whether or not they trust you. Be authentic, transparent, vulnerable, and above all trustworthy.

Clients want lawyers who are leaders and champions *for them*. When you create "know you, like you, trust you" relationships, you create the foundation for sourcing and creating your own clients.

PUBLIC SPEAKING

One of the best ways to brand yourself as a thought leader is to speak at venues and events where your ideal clients are present. Being seen on a regular basis increases your visibility and acceptance by others. Clients want lawyers who understand their concerns and challenges.

CLIENT RETENTION, REPEAT BUSINESS, AND REFERRALS

The cost of acquiring a new client will usually be greater than receiving repeat business and referrals. Cost-effective means retaining clients and receiving referrals from clients and others.

- Create touch points because out of sight generally means out of mind. Publish email or print newsletters offering updates on relevant topics or court decisions.
- Hold luncheons in your conference room with other experts.

LEAD GENERATION

A lead is an investment. The best way to create leads is to consistently brand your credibility, expertise, and experience. Lead generation is a contact sport where you get the opportunity to share your brand and message.

LEAD TRACKING

Tracking leads and opportunities is critical to turning investments into income. Track everything. You never know where your next client will come from. Segment leads into hot, warm and cold categories. Leads can also be segmented into potential clients and centers of influence.

LEAD CLOSING

A lead conversion is a return on your investment. Closings happen when you help clients identify problems and provide evidence that you can solve them. Closings also happen when you eliminate the fear clients have of making a wrong decision.

REFERRALS

Let referral sources know exactly what your ideal client looks like. Tell your referral sources why someone should hire you. Find ways to reciprocate with referral sources. Learn who *their* ideal clients are.

SOCIAL MEDIA

Social Media can be your virtual showroom showcasing all your services and value proposition. The right social media can be used to position you as an expert and thought leader. In the fast moving world of social media, thought leaders and rainmakers keep a pulse on the news and culture of society. Some thought leaders maintain blogs and voice their opinions through social media. As a result, they are often quoted and reinforced as thought leaders.

SEARCH ENGINE OPTIMIZATION (SEO)

More and more prospects conduct Google searches before they agree to a first meeting. Make sure that every channel is consistent and delivers the message you want your customers to read. A few "party pictures" on your Facebook page can cost you a fortune in lost business. If you were your ideal client, would your social media presence create likability and build trust and confidence in you?

Channels include:

- Website
- Blog
- Facebook
- LinkedIn
- Pinterest
- Instagram
- Twitter
- Periscope
- YouTube
- Bylined email articles and E-zines
- Virtual Seminars

GOAL SETTING

- Set specific goals for how many clients or how much revenue you want to generate. Don't try to bring in "as may clients as possible." Calculate your capacity and then make plans to grow, refine your client profile, or both.
- Develop a realistic timeline for these goals.
- Focus on what support you will need to accomplish your specified goals.
- Deliver a clear, powerful message of your value proposition.
- Be able to deliver your message in 60 seconds or less.

BUDGETS

Marketing budgets can range from 5% to 10% or more of your gross income. Expenses can include:

- Social events
- Sporting events
- Charitable events
- Business or trade events
- Breakfast, lunch or dinner events
- Newsletters
- Social media
- Website
- (CRM) Customer Relationship Management

COMPENSATION MODELS

A marketing plan should clearly define who and how partners and associates get compensated for bringing in clients. State Bar Associations usually publish specific guidelines and limitations governing commission and compensation practices. Don't reinvent the wheel only to end up with a flat tire.

- How are origination credits valued and whose client is it?
- How long will the origination credit continue for each client?
- Who determines if a case will be billed hourly, will be flat fee based, or a combination?
- If an attorney who works on your case gets a referral, whose origination is it?
- Is the value of one billable hour greater than or equal to one business development hour?

COMMUNITY INVOLVEMENT

Community involvement is not about attending functions and working rooms. Everyone knows what an inauthentic, event-darting networker looks like. When you attend events, get there early. Look at all the attendee nametags, decide who you would like to meet, and then stand at the front door to greet and identify attendees.

If you don't recognize a company's name or a representative's name, Google them and decide if they would be worthwhile to connect with. Look at the nametags again to determine whom you think *they* might want to meet. Very often, I meet and greet by taking a new person with me and introducing him or her to my contacts.

People will make snap judgments about you based on what they see, hear, and sense about you. When you walk into a room, it's show time and you are on stage. Stay focused on why you are there.

Recommendations for creating lifetime relationships and clients:

- Leave your ego at the door.
- Get there early
- Have fun
- Say "hello" first and state your name clearly and slowly
- Look people in the eye and connect with them
- Always stand when being introduced
- Be involved
- Be interested
- Be brief

- Don't interrupt
- Be a connector worker
- Be a note taker
- Don't give your business card out until you have permission or a request for it.
- Follow up within 48 hours
- Don't accept a call unless it is an emergency when in the middle of a conversation.

As a lawyer, you create your ongoing employment by generating revenue.

- Being self-generating and self-supporting can be lonely, scary and uncertain. Be more motivated by the power that comes with having control of your destiny than by your fear.
- You are either an employee of someone else or an employer of yourself. To become an employer, you must have an owner's mindset. Self-generating people always have an owner's mindset.
- When you train for a sporting event or a career, there comes a time when you must get on the court and compete. When you are the employer, you are always competing.

SUMMARY

Origination leaders know what they have to offer customers and clients.

Building a practice is about being a leader.

When leadership is present, client acquisitions are easier.

Clients want lawyers who can solve their problems through leadership.

Leaders have brands.

The rainmaker inside of you can be your brand.

Your brand is your promise.

Your brand differentiates you from other attorneys.

You brand is derived from:

- Who you aspire to be for your clients.
- Who your clients perceive you to be for them.

Others will judge you by what you say and what you don't say. They will also judge you by how you say it and why you say it. Be thoughtful and authentic in all of your communications.

Clients want lawyers who are:

> Credible
>
> Clear
>
> Concerned
>
> Concise

Consistent

Committed

ACTION PLAN SUMMARY

- Create an ideal client profile.
- Identify the best places to meet ideal clients.
- Be able to clearly verbalize your unique value proposition.
- Create a follow-up process for keeping in touch with ideal clients.
- Create new distribution outlets for your firm's services.

When you attempt to be branded for *everything*, you run the risk of not being branded for *anything*. Your brand is not your brochure; it is *you*. Once you, your values, your commitments, your personality, and your expertise are a brand, create a consistent tagline, message, and voice.

The only person you can count on is *you*. Be self-reliant. Attorneys create income; business originators create *wealth*.

You may have read this book the first time out of curiosity. Now read this book *again* knowing you can originate clients by finding the rainmaker inside you.

THE SECRET SAUCE IS NOT A SECRET

You do not have to have your own law practice to have an owner's mindset and become a successful business originator. Cultivate an attitude, conviction, and desire to be a leader. Have a say in your career development and destiny.

Progressive law firms create leadership tracks for young and entrepreneurial lawyers. If they don't, they risk losing their leaders to more progressive law firms. Leading lawyers position themselves to establish their own successful practices inside their groups once they have clients. Origination development is really about attorney leadership development.

Lawyers who have a practice "do business"; lawyers who have clients "have a business."

The collective energy of attorneys dedicated to learning how to create and grow a legal business is powerful. Participants see themselves in other lawyers who are working through there own process of creating a brand and strategy. Success stories of others provide confidence that they can do it also. Lawyers begin to see how they can give and receive referrals from each other. Confidence grows as skills are learned, honed and tested.

To learn more about business development workshops and coaching programs, visit Howard on the web at *lawyersrainingclients.com*

FIND THE RAINMAKER INSIDE YOU

ABOUT THE AUTHOR

Howard Wolkowitz is an energetic and creative visionary. In High School, he wanted to go to business college to learn about the world of business. He majored in industrial psychology so he could learn how people relate and work in a business setting. In graduate school, he majored in business management.

When Howard started his working career in 1974, events created a professional pathway. It took three jobs before Howard realized he could create his own life as an entrepreneur.

On his kitchen table, he created two businesses. In 1987, he sold one of the businesses to a Fortune 100 company. After his employment contract ended in 1992, Howard decided to create another new business in the financial services industry. 23 years later, Howard is still creating. A new book and seminar series shares the valuable lessons he has learned over the last 40+ years.

www.ingramcontent.com/pod-product-compliance
Lightning Source LLC
Chambersburg PA
CBHW032021190326
41520CB00007B/569